Copyright © 2008 by Mary F. Pecci

All rights reserved.
No part of this book may be reproduced
without written consent of the author.

FIRST EDITION

ISBN NO. 0-943220-16-5

Distributed by:

PECCI EDUCATIONAL PUBLISHERS
440 Davis Court, No. 405
San Francisco, CA 94111-2400

Tel: (415) 391- 8579 - E-mail: mpecci@sbcglobal.net

www.OnlineReadingTeacher.com

Other books by Mary F. Pecci:

Pre-Primers I, II, III
SUPER SEATWORK - Content Areas
SUPER SEATWORK - Letter- Recognition
SUPER SEATWORK - Linguistic Exercises
SUPER SEATWORK - Word Skills
SUPER SEATWORK - Color Words
SUPER SEATWORK - Number Words
SUPER SEATWORK - Phonic Grab Bag

How to Discipline Your Class For Joyful Teaching!

SUPER SPELLING - Book One

Why Johnny Ain't NEVER Gonna Read!
(A Challenge to the Nation)

This Primer is designed to be used in correlation with:

At Last! A Reading Method for EVERY Child!

Written by: Mary F. Pecci, Reading Specialist
Edited by: Ernest F. Pecci, Child Psychiatrist

ACKNOWLEDGMENTS

This reading series is dedicated to my beloved brother, Dr. Ernest F. Pecci, and his remarkable daughter, Diana Pecci La Brecque, who set this project into motion by saying those magic words, "Yes! You CAN do it!"

Sincere appreciation also goes to my sister, Marguerite Pecci Kelley, for her story suggestions and for always being on call to backboard ideas.

And a very special thanks goes to June Triesch, quintessential Kindergarten teacher, who retired on her 80th birthday, about whom such teachers it has been written, "God doesn't have hands; He uses the teacher's hands," for taking on the role of story editor, for contributing her own story ideas, and for her constant faithfulness over the years as dearest friend and mentor.

Teacher's Guide

Pages p. 121 -143

Vocabulary Word List:
> Part I - p. 121-122
> Part II - p. 131-132

Word-for-Word Dialogue between Teacher and Student:
> Part I - p. 123-130
> Part II - p. 133-143

In this reader, about 215 words are formally introduced. However, reading vocabulary will not be limited to these words because students will be acquiring independent decoding skills as they progress through this reader. This reader serves only as a springboard, from which students will be able to read *any* material on (and in most cases above) their academic level.

Stop and Go

This is Bobby.
Bobby is not a big boy.
He is just a little boy.

"Mom," said Bobby.
"Can we go for a walk?
I want to go for a walk now."

Mother said, "We can go for a walk, Bobby.
We can go for a walk now."

"You can walk fast, Mom," said Bobby.
"You can walk fast, fast, fast!"

"I can walk fast, Bobby," said Mother.

"I can walk fast, too," said Bobby.
"I can walk fast, too."

"Oh, Bobby," said Mother.
"You can walk fast, too.
You are not little. You are a big boy now."

"Look, Bobby!" said Mother.
"Look! Do you see that big red 🚦?

We can not walk fast now.
We have to stop for a big red 🚦."

"Oh, Mom," said Bobby.
"Do we have to stop for the big red 🚦 now?"

Mother said, "We have to stop now.
We have to stop for a big red 🚦."

"Look, Mom," said Bobby.
"We can not walk fast now.
I see a big red 🚩."

"Oh, Bobby," said Mother.
"You are a funny boy.
We do not have to stop for a big red 🚩.
We just have to stop for a big red 🚦."

"Oh, I see," said Bobby.
"We just have to stop for the big red 🚦."

"Look at that little 🐢, Dad," said Bobby.
"A 🐢 can not walk fast.
It can walk slow. Slow, slow, slow.

I want to have a little 🐢 to play with, Dad.
Will you get a little 🐢 for me?"

"We must ask Mother," said Dad.
"I will have to talk with her."

"Will you talk with Mom now?" said Bobby.

"Mom, Bobby wants to have a little 🐢 to play with," said Father.

"Can we get a little 🐢 for Bobby?"

Mother said, "Bobby can have a little 🐢 to play with. We must go to see them at the pet 🏠."

"Oh, Mom!" said Bobby. "I want to see them now! I want to talk to them!"

Father said, "We will walk to the pet 🏠."

"Just look at them walk!" said Bobby.
"They walk slow, slow, slow."

"Get a 🐢 that will come to you, Bobby," said Mother.

"You must ask a 🐢 to come to you," said Father. "You must talk to them."

"Come to me little 🐢 ," said Bobby.
"I want to play with you.

Do you want to come with me?"

"This little 🐢 is looking at me.
See him stop to look at me," said Bobby.

"Now, that little 🐢 is looking at me.
I will ask them to come to me now."

"Come to me little 🐢 🐢," said Bobby.

"Oh, look at them come to me!

I want to have this little 🐢 AND that little 🐢, too! Can I have them?"

"We will get them for you," said Mom.

"Oh boy!" said Bobby. "This is fun!"

The Lost ✂

"Bob," said Mother.
"I can not find my red ✂. Did you see it?
I must find it. I want to cut this 🔷."

"I did not see it, Pat," said Father.
"Did you ask Bobby? You must ask him."

"I must find him," said Mother.
"Did you ask him to go out to play?"

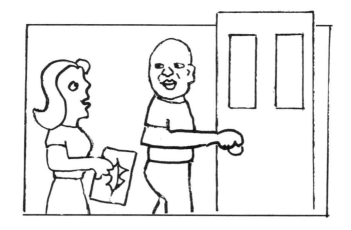

"I did ask him to go out to play," said Father. "I will walk out and look for him. I will find him and talk with him."

"Good," said Mother.
"Ask him to help us find the lost red ✂."

"He did not come out to play," said Father.
"I must look for him in the 🏠."

In and out.
In and out.

"I see Bobby's red ball," said Father.
"I see his little red 🚗 , too.
He is in the 🏠. I must find him.
I must ask him to help find the lost ✂ ."

"Oh, oh," said Father.
"Just look at that 🦐. Is that fur?
This is not good. I must find Bobby.
I must find him fast!"

"Look at me!" said Bobby.
"I am a big, big boy!
I can cut with the red ✂. Cut, cut, cut.
I look good. Good, good, good!"

"Oh, Bob," said Mother.
"You did find my lost ✂.
And you did find Bobby, too."

"You must NOT do that!" said Father.
"Oh, oh," said Bobby. "I must NOT do that!"

Lost and Found

"What did you find, Bobby?" asked Mother.

"I found this little 🧸, Mom," said Bobby.
"Now it is for me."

"No, no, Bobby," said Mother.
"It is lost. It is not for you.
We must go to the Lost and Found now."

"What is this?"
asked Bobby.

"Give it to me, Bobby," said Mother.
"See what I do now."

"Hi!, I am Little .
I can walk.
I can talk, too.
I can walk slow.
I can walk fast.
I can jump up.
I can jump down, too!"

"Oh, my!" said Bobby.
"What a funny, funny little .
Just see it walk and talk.
It can jump up and down, too"

"Look, Bobby," said Mother.
"Do you see that baby at the Lost and Found? He must have lost this little 🐻.
This little 🐻 is his.
We must give it to him."

"No, no," said Bobby.
"I do not want to give it to that baby.
I want it for me."

"I am for Baby Boy.
I am for Baby Boy.
I am for Baby Boy,"
said little 🐻.

" said Bobby.

e 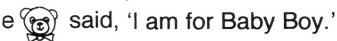 said, 'I am for Baby Boy.'

This little I found is not for me.
I will give it to Baby Boy."

"What a good boy you are," said Mother.
"You will give the you found to Baby Boy.

Now I will go out and get a little for you.

"Oh, good!" said Bobby.
"If it is lost, it can find me.
It will just talk and say,
"I am for Bobby!"

Bobby ran to Father.
"Dad!" said Bobby.
"Do you want to see what I can do?"

"What can you do?" asked Father.

"I can say the ABC's," said Bobby. "Look - A - B - C - D - H - K - L."

"Oh, no," said Father.
"I must help you.
Go back to the D.
When you get to the D, you say, E - F - G."

Bobby said, "A - B - C - D - E - F - G - Q - T - R - L - P."

17

"Why do you want to say the ABC's?" asked Dad. "You are too little."

"No, no," said Bobby. "I can do it. I am big - A - B - C - D - L - K - X."

"Stop now," said Father. "We must go out and walk to the toy  to find a toy to help."

"What toy?" asked Bobby.

"A toy that will talk to you," said Father.

"Why must the toy talk to me?" asked Bobby.

"You will see," said Father.

"See all the ABC toys, Bobby?" asked Father. "Which toy do you want? All of them can help you to say the ABC's."

"I want that toy," said Bobby.

"Just do this and it will talk to you," said Father.

"This toy can talk slow. This toy can talk fast. When we get back to the 🏠, you must play with it."

"This is fun!" said Bobby.

Bobby did play with the toy. He did it and he did it and he did it.

Then he ran to Father and said, "Dad, ask me to say the ABC's."

Father said, "Will you say the ABC's?"

Bobby said, "A - B - C - D - E - F - G . . ."

"Go, Bobby, Go!" said Father.

"H - I - J - K - L - M - N - O - P," said Bobby.

"Good, Bobby," said Father. "Go, go, go!"

"Q - R - S - T - U - V . . . ," said Bobby.

"You can do it," said Father. "Go, go go!"

Bobby said, "W - X . . . - Y - Z. I did it! I did it! I can say the ABC's! I AM big now!"

A Dog for Bobby

"Stop, Dad," said Bobby.
"Do you see that little dog?
It must be lost.
I want it to come to live with us."

"Yes, I see the little dog," said Father.
"We must find out if it *is* lost.
If it is lost, then it can come to live with us."

"How will we find out if the dog is lost?" asked Bobby.

"We will walk up and down the ===== and ask," said Father.

Father found out that the dog was lost.

Then Bobby said, "Yes! Now you can come to live with us, little dog!"

When he was back at the 🏠, Bobby said, "It will be fun to tell my dog how to do what I ask him to do.

"When I say, 'Sit,' I want him to sit.
When I say, 'Stand,' I want him to stand."

"Yes," said Father.
"That will be fun."

Bobby looked at the dog and said, "Sit."

He said it slow.
He said it fast.

The dog did not sit.

Bobby looked at the dog and said, "Stand."

He said it slow.
He said it fast.

The dog did not stand.

"Oh, no," said Bobby.
"Be a good dog.
What can I do now?"

He ran to Father and asked, "Can you tell me why my dog will not do what I ask him to do?"

Father said, "Yes, I will tell you why. You must let him see this 🍿.

Then say, 'Sit.'

"If he will sit, then give him the 🍿. If he will not sit, then do not give it to him."

Bobby did what Father said.
He did it, and he did it, and he did it.

The dog looked, and he looked, and he looked.

      Then - the dog DID sit.

"Yes!" said Bobby. "Good dog, good dog! Now I will find out if he will stand when I say, 'Stand.'"

Did the dog stand?
Yes, he did!

Spell The Word

"I see Tom," said Jan.
"That boy is a good speller. Bill is with him. He is a good speller, too. I will ask them to play 'Spell The Word' with me."

"Hi, Tom. Hi, Bill," said Jan.
"Do you want to play 'Spell The Word'?"

"Yes," said Tom.
"Yes," said Bill.

"'Spell The Word' will help us to be a good speller," said Jan.

"And it is fun, too," said Tom.
"Let us do it!" said Bill.

Jan said, "When I give you a word to spell, you have to spell it fast.

The boy that can spell the word fast will get a ★.

The boy that can get all the ★★ will be the best speller."

"Good," said Tom."

"Go, girl, go!" said Bill.

"Who can spell the word 'dog'?" said Jan.

Tom was slow.
Bill was fast. He said,

"D - O - G"

"Yes! Good!" said Jan.
"Let me give you a ★."

"Now, who can spell the word 'cat'?" said Jan.

Tom was slow.
Bill was fast. He said,

"C - A - T"

"Yes! Good!" said Jan.
"Let me give you a ★."

"Who can spell the word 'fish'?" said Jan.

Tom was slow.
Bill was fast. He said,

"F - I - S - H"

"Yes! Good!" said Jan."
"Let me give you a ★."

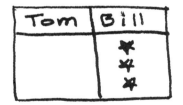

"Oh, my," said Tom. "How do you do it? Why are you so good at 'Spell The Word'?"

Bill said, "I just sound out the word. That is how I do it."

"Oh, I see," said Jan. "Now I will give you a word that you can *not* sound out."

"Oh, no!" said Tom.
"Oh, yes!" said Jan.
"Who can spell the word ?"

Tom did not say a word.
Bill did not say a word.

Then Bill said, "I can do it -

B-I-C-Y-C-L-E"

"Yes!" said Jan. What a good speller you are! How did you do it?"

Bill did not say a word.

Then Jan looked out the

"Oh, I see how you did it," said Jan.
"That is not funny."

"Now who is the best speller?" asked Tom.

"I am," said Bill, "if Jan will give us just words that I can sound out."

"Hi, Bill," said Tom. "Dad and I are going to Fun Park. Do you want to come with us?"

"I will have to go and ask my Mom if I can come with you," said Bill.

"Run fast and come back," said Tom.

When Bill was back, he said, "She said 'yes,' I can come with you."

"Good!" said Tom.
"Look! There is our bus.
The bus will start now."

"Where is Fun Park?" asked Bill.

"You will see," said Tom.

The bus went on and on.

Then Father said, "Look! There it is! There is Fun Park! Let us get off the bus now."

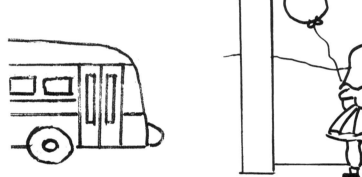

"Good!" said Bill.
"I want to see what is there at Fun Park."

"We will have much fun at Fun Park," said Tom.

"Let us run to the park.
We will have much fun there.
Let us run fast to the park."

"Just look at the boy and girl there," said Bill.
"She is going up and he is going down.
Just look at her. Just look at him.
What fun that must be for them."

"Look there!" said Tom.

"Where?" asked Bill.

"There," said Tom.
"Do you see the little red cars there?"

"Yes, I see them," said Bill.

"I will tell my Dad that we are going on the little red cars," said Tom.
"We will have much fun there!"

"Do you see what I see?" asked Tom.

"What is that?" said Bill.
"Look at all that fur."

"See what I do," said Tom.

"Oh, my!" said Bill. "You look funny with all that fur. Will you be my pet?"

"No," said Tom. I am not a pet. I just have fur."

"Let me do it now," said Bill. "This is much fun!"

"Now look at you, Bill," said Tom.
"Now you have fur and you look funny."

"Oh, oh," said Father. "Our bus is back. There it is. It will start to go now. Let us get back on the bus."

"We did have much fun at Fun Park, Dad," said Tom. "Did you have fun at Fun Park, Bill?"

"Yes, I had much fun at Fun Park," said Bill.

"How much fun did you have?" asked Tom.

"THIS MUCH!" said Bill.

"We will have to come back to Fun Park," said Father. "Now let us run back to the bus."

Scout

"I want to go for a walk to the big park," said Bobby.

He did not ask his mother.
He did not ask his father.
He just went out the

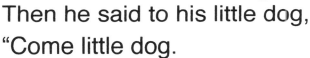

Then he said to his little dog,
"Come little dog.
We will start to walk to the big park. It will be fun to go there."

"Bow-wow," said his little dog.

And off went Bobby and his little dog to the big park.

Bobby went this way.
Bobby went that way.
He did not find the park.

He looked this way.
He looked that way.
The park was not there.

"Where, oh where, is the park?" said Bobby. "I can not find the park, little dog. Let us go back to our  ."

Bobby went this way.
Bobby went that way.
He did not find the way back to his .

"Where, oh where, is our 🏠?" said Bobby. "How can we find the way back? We are lost. This is not much fun at all."

Then Bobby said, "I see a bus. I will ask the man on the bus to help us. He will tell us which way to go.

"Stop! Stop, bus!" said Bobby. "We are lost and we want you to help us find our way back to our 🏠!"

The bus did not stop there. It just went by. The man on the bus did not see Bobby and his little dog.

"Good-by, bus," said Bobby. "Oh, my! I wish I had asked my Mom and Dad to let me go out to the park.

'Who will help us now? What can we do?"

Just then, his little dog got up and said, "Bow-wow." Then he ran down the =====.

"Come back little dog," said Bobby. He ran to get his little dog.

"Where are you going, little dog?" said Bobby. "Come back! Come back!"

The dog just ran and ran and ran. Bobby ran and ran too.

Then - what did Bobby see?

Can it be? Yes! It CAN be. It was his !

"Oh, my," said Bobby to his little dog. "You found the way back to our big . What a good dog you are! Good dog!"

When Bobby got back, his father said, "Bobby, do not go out if you do not ask us. You must NOT do that!"

"I wanted to walk to the big park." said Bobby. "I did not find the way there. I just got lost. Then I did not find the way back.

"My little dog found the way back. He can tell which way to go to find our He can find the way back the way a boy scout can. That is why I will call him 'Scout.'"

"Bow-wow! Bow-wow!" said Scout.

We Play with Clay

"What is that?" asked Tom.

"It is clay," said Bill.

"Where did you get it?" asked Tom.

"My Dad got it for me," said Bill.
"See what I can do with it."

This hand went in and out of the clay.
That hand went in and out of the clay.
This way and that way.
This way and that way.

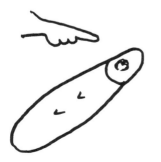

Then he said, "What do you see there? Can you tell me what that is?"

"Is it a ✏️?" asked Tom.
"No, no. It is not a ✏️," said Bill.

"Is it a fish?" asked Tom.

"Yes. It is a fish," said Billl.
"See my fish swim slow.
See my fish swim fast."

"You are funny, Bill," said Tom.
"I wish I had clay to play with."

"I will let you play with
my clay," said Bill.
"I want to see what
you can do with it."

This hand went in and out of the clay.
That hand went in and out of the clay.
This way and that way.
This way an that way.

Then he said, "Can you
tell me what this is?"

"Is it a car?" asked Bill?
"No, no. It is not a car," said Tom.

"Is it a bus?" asked Bill.

"Yes. It is a bus," said Tom.
"See my bus go slow.
See my bus go fast.
Go, bus go!

See where my bus is going," said Tom.

This hand went in and out of the clay.
That hand went in and out of the clay.
This way and that way.
This way and that way.

Then he said, "See this clay house? My bus is going to this clay house."

"Is there a family in that clay house?"
asked Bill.

"No. There is no family in there.
It is too little.
This is a dog house for Scout," said Tom.

"Oh," said Bill. "Now let me have the clay. You will see what I can do for Scout."

This hand went in and out of the clay.
That hand went in and out of the clay.
This way and that way.
This way and that way.

Then he said, "Can you tell me what it is?"

"Yes," said Tom. It is a 🦴."

Just then, Scout ran by and looked at the 🦴.

"Do not get that 🦴!" said Tom.

But Scout got the 🦴 and looked at them.

"Do not start to run with that 🦴, Scout," said Bill.
But Scout did start to run with the 🦴 in his 👅.

"Come back, Scout. Come back!" said Tom.

"Come back when we call you," said Bill. "That is not a 🦴. It is just clay."

But Scout did not want to give the clay 🦴 back to them. He just ran into the big house with the clay 🦴.

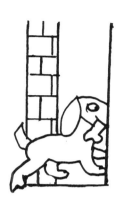

When he did come out of the big house, this is how he looked.

"Oh, my!" said Bill.
"Oh, no!" said Tom.

Just look at Scout now.

Did Scout want the clay 🦴 now?
Not at all.

Did Scout say, "Bow-wow?"

No. He did not.
Why not?
There was too much clay in his .

Who is Happy Now?

Jan was walking to the park with her doll.
What did she see?

A little duck.

"Hello, little duck," she said.

"Are you lost?
Do you want to live in my house with me?"

The little duck said, "Quack, quack."
But the little duck did not look happy.

Tom was walking to the park, too.
He had his toy truck with him.

What did he see?

A little frog.

"Hello, little frog," he said.

"Are you lost?
Do you want to live in my house with me?"

The little frog jumped up and down.
But the little frog did not look happy.

Jan and Tom met at the park.

"Where did you get that duck?" asked Tom.

"I found it on the way to the park," said Jan. "It must be lost. Where did you get that frog?"

"I found it on the way to the park, too," said Tom. "It must be lost."

Just then, what did Jan see?
A duck family swim by.

"Oh! Look, Tom," she said.

"Do you see what I see?"

"Yes! I see a duck family swim by," said Tom. "It must be the family of little duck."

Little duck said, "Quack, quack."

"Oh, my!" said Jan.
"What can I do now?
What is best for little duck?
Is it best for little duck to come to live with me?
Is it best for little duck to go back to her family?"

Then, what did Tom see?
A frog family jump by.

"Look, Jan!" he said.
"Do you see what I see?"

"Yes!" said Jan.
"I see a frog family jump by.
It must be the family of little frog.
See little frog jump up and down."

"Oh, my!" said Tom.
"What can I do now?
What is best for little frog?
Is it best for little frog to
come to live with me?
Is it best for little frog to
go back to his family?"

 Jan looked at Tom.
Tom looked at Jan.

"I wish I had a pet duck," said Jan.
"But I can have fun with my little doll.
I will give little duck back to her family.
Good-by, little duck."

"I wish I had a pet frog," said Tom.
"But I can play with my toy truck.
I will give little frog back to his family.
Good-by, little frog."

WHO IS HAPPY NOW?

Little duck is happy.
The duck family is happy.
Little frog is happy. The frog family is happy.
And Jan and Tom are happy too!

The Play House

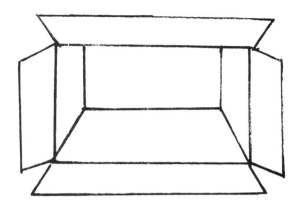

On the way to the park, Bill saw a big box.

"Oh," he said. "I wish I had a play house.
That big box can be a good play house.
I will call my best friend, Tom.
I will ask him to help me work on this box.
It is a good day to do it."

"Hello, Tom," said Bill.
"I wish we had a play
house to have fun in.

I found a big box today.
If we work on it, it will
be a good play house.

You are my best friend.
Will you help me work on it?"

"Yes," said Tom. "You are my best friend, too, and I wish we had a play house to have fun in. I will come there with my toy car and a 🏠 for the play house."

"Good!" said Bill. "I will get my toy truck and a 🏠, too. We will work and work and then have fun in it."

When they met, Bill said, "See how big that box is?
We can sit in it.
We can stand in it."

"Wow," said Bill.
"Let us start to work on it now."

Bill and Tom did work and work and work. By and by, the play house did look good.

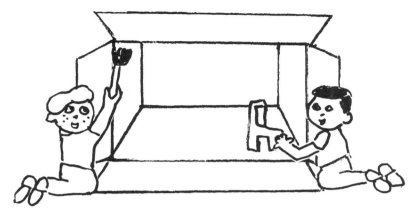

Bill said, "We can live in our play house today. We will be happy in our play house."

Jan and Beth went by.

"Hello, boys," said Jan. "May we come in your play house? It must be fun to play in there."

"Oh, no," said Bill. "You are a good friend, but no girl can come in our play house. This play house is just for boys. Good-by, girls."

"Oh, Beth," said Jan.
"I wish we had a play house, too.
What can we do?"

Then Beth saw where Bill got his big box.

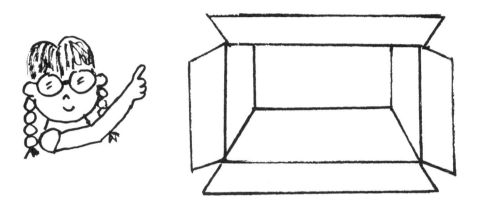

"Look there!" said Beth.
"Do you see what I see?
This is where Bill got his big box.
We can get a big box, too."

"Yes!" said Jan.
"It will be a good play house for us.

Let us start to work on it now."

The girls did work and work and work.
The play house did look good.

"I will get my doll family," said Beth.
"My mother doll, father doll, and baby doll.
What can you get for our play house?"

"I will get my little 🛋 and my mother will give us 🍪🍪🍪," said Jan.

"It will be fun to live in our play house.
We will be happy in our play house today."

By and by, the boys went by.
"Look at the play house the girls have," said Tom. "Let us ask them if we can go in the play house with them and get a 🍪."

"Hello, girls!" said Tom.
"May we come in your play house?"

"You are a good friend," said Jan,
"but no boy can come in our play house.
This play house is just for girls.
Good-by, boys!"

Then Scout went by.
He said, "Bow-wow!
Bow-wow!"

Scout is not a boy.
Scout is not a girl.

Did Jan and Beth let Scout in the play house?

Did Scout get a ?

Yes, and yes!

Fly, Bird, Fly

Pete and Tom went for a bike ride to the park. On the way, Pete looked up at a big 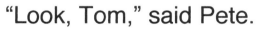.   What did he see?

He saw a mother bird and a little baby bird.

"Look, Tom," said Pete.
"Look up there in that big 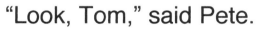.
Do you see that mother bird and her baby bird? It must be time for the baby bird to start to fly."

"Yes, I see them," said Tom.
The mother bird wants her little baby bird to fly out of the nest. But it will not fly. It will not fly out of the nest."

"Oh, no!" said Pete.
"Now look at the baby bird.
It will fall out of the nest!
If the mother bird can not
help it, how can we help?"

"Get on your bike, Pete," said Tom,
"and start to ride fast to the baby bird.
You can help the baby bird if you let it fal
in your hand."

Pete got on his bike and did start to ride
fast. Just in time, the little baby bird did fall
in his hand.

"Oh, good!" said Tom.
"You *did* help the little baby bird.
May I pet him now?"

"Yes, you may," said Pete.
"He is a good little bird."

"Hello, little bird," said Tom.
"You are a good little bird.
But it is time for you to start to fly.
Then you will not fall out of your nest."

But just then, the mother bird saw Tom.
What did she do? She did start to fly at
Tom. She was not happy. No, not at all.
She wanted her little baby bird back.

"Oh, no!" said Pete
to the mother bird.
"Tom is your friend.
I am your friend.

We just want to help your little baby bird.
We will get him back in the nest for you."

Pete got off of his bike and got on Tom.

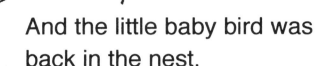

And the little baby bird was back in the nest.

"Good-by little bird," said Pete.
"Good-by little bird," said Tom.

Now the mother bird is happy.
Pete and Tom are happy too.

"You are a good friend to the baby bird and mother bird," said Pete. "And you are a good friend to them, too," said Tom.

"Yes," said Pete.
"And it was much fun to help them today."

"The next time we see them," said Tom, "we will see that little bird fly."

"Yes," said Pete. "We will see that little bird fly - - - way, way up in the sky."

How to Get the Job Done

"Come here, Beth," said her mother. "There is much work to be done in this house today. I want your help to get it done."

"What do you want me to do?" asked Beth.

"I want you to make your bed," said her mother. "Do you know how to make your bed?"

"Yes, I know how to make my bed," said Beth. "But do I have to do it now? I am on my way to play with my friend, Jan."

"Yes, you *do* have to make your bed now," said her mother. "Start now. Here is why -

> **I** have a job to do.
> **You** have a job to do.
> **Together**, we get the job done!"

"Come here, Steve," said his mother. "There is much work to be done in this house today. I want your help to get it done."

"What do you want me to do?" asked Steve.

"I want you to walk the dog," said his mother. "I do not want him in this house while I work. Do you know how to walk the dog?"

"Yes, I know how to walk the dog," said Steve. "But do I have to do it now? I am on my way to play with my friend, Bill."

"Yes, you *do* have to walk the dog now," said his mother. "Start now. Here is why -

>**I** have a job to do.
>**You** have a job to do.
>**Together**, we get the job done!"

While Beth did a good job on her bed, Steve was out for a walk with the dog.

But the dog wanted to play with his 🦴 in the house. Steve did not have the dog 🪢 with him. The dog started to run back to the house.

"Come here," said Steve. "Come here now!"

But the dog did not do what Steve said.

Beth was done with her work, and she wanted to go out to play with her friend, Jan. But the dog came in and started to jump up and down on her bed.

Just then her mother came by and saw the bed.

"Why is your job not done?" she asked.
"Did you forget what I said to you? -

I have a job to do.
You have a job to do.
Together, we get the job done."

"I did not forget," said Jan.
"I did make my bed. The job was all done. But the dog came in and jumped on the bed."

Just then, Steve came in.

Mother said to him, "Steve, did I tell you to walk the dog while I work in the house? Did you forget what I said to you? -

I have a job to do.
You have a job to do.
Together, we get the job done."

"I did not forget," said Steve.
"I came back to get the ."

"The next time you walk the dog, get the  and *then* go for the walk," said his mother. "Do you and Beth know *why* I want you to do your job?"

"Yes, I know, I know!" said Steve.
"Yes, I know, I know!" said Beth.

"**I** have a job to do.

You have a job to do.

Together, we get the job done!"

The New Game

"Hello, Steve and Tom," said Pam and Kim. "Do you want to play a new game with us?"

"What is the name of the new game?" asked Steve.

"The name of the new game is 'Make a Rhyme,'" said Pam.

"How do you play Make a Rhyme?" asked Tom.

"I give you a sentence.

Then you have to give me a sentence that will rhyme with the last word in my sentence," said Kim.

"What is a rhyme?" asked Steve.

"A rhyme is a word with the same sound at the end of the word that I have at the end of my word," said Pam.

"Just see how we play the new game and then you can do it," said Kim.

    Kim: I like to play this new **game**.
    Pam: It is fun and I like the **name**.

"Oh, I see," said Steve. "The last word in my sentence must rhyme with the last word in your sentence."

"Yes," said Pam. "You have it! Now can you start to play Make a Rhyme with us?"

"Yes! Here we go," said Tom.

Steve: This is a new game I **like**.
Tom: Now go for a ride on your **bike**.

"Good job! Good job" said Pam and Kim. "We like the way you boys play Make a Rhyme."

"Now you go, girls," said Steve.

Pam: I like to do my **best**.
Kim: When I have a big **test**.

"This is fun!" said Tom. "I like this new game."

"Now you go, boys," said Pam.

Tom: The man did not go to the **park**.
Steve: He did not want to see a **shark**.

"But there is no shark in the park," said Kim.

"I know," said Steve. "But it is a rhyme."

"Now you go, girls," said Tom.

Kim: What do you want for a **wish**?
Pam: I want to have a funny **fish**.

"This is fun," said Steve. "But this will have to be the last game for us today. We have to go home and get our work done."

"Make your last game good," said Pam.

Steve: We are happy that we **came**.
Tom: We like to play this new **game**.

"Good-by, boys," said Kim and Pam. "We want to play this new game the next time we see **you**."

"Good-by, girls," said Tom and Steve. "We want to play this new game the next time we see you, **too**!"

Let's Trade

Steve went in his room and looked at his old toys. He saw toys he had not played with for a while.

He said, "It is time I got new toys.
But my mom and dad said, 'Not now.'
I wish I had new toys today.
What can I do?"

After a while, he said, "I know what I can do. I can start a 'Let's Trade' game today.

I will take all of my old toys
and put them in a box. Then I
will call all of my best friends
and tell them to come here
with old toys."

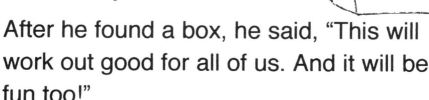

After he found a box, he said, "This will work out good for all of us. And it will be fun too!"

After a while, Bill and Pete came by with old toys.

"Hello, Steve," said Bill and Pete. "Why did you want us to take all of our old toys here?"

"I will tell you why after Bob and Tom get here," said Steve.

After a while, Bob and Tom got there.

"Hello, Steve," said Bob and Tom. "Why did you want us to take all of our old toys here?"

"I will tell all of you why," said Steve. "We are going to play a new game you will like. The name of the game is 'Let's Trade.'"

"How do you play that new game?" asked Bill.

"Here is how you play the 'Let's Trade' game," said Steve.

"You put an old toy in this box. Then you take the toy you like best out of this box."

"Oh, I see," said Bill. "Your old toy will be our new toy."

"Yes, you are right," said Steve. "Now we can play the new game. It will be fun. You may start, Bob.

Let's trade! Put an old toy in.
Take a new toy out.
Put and take.
Put and take."

"Here I go," said Bob.
He put his old toy in the box. "Now I will take a toy I like out of the box."

After he did this, he said, "You are right," Steve. This new game *is* fun. And I like my new toy, too!"

"Am I next?" asked Tom.

"That is right. You are next," said Steve.

> "**Let's trade**! Put an old toy in.
> Take a new toy out.
> Put and take.
> Put and take."

Tom put an old toy in the box and got a new toy out of the box. He was happy with it, too.

"You go next, Pete," said Steve.

> "**Let's trade!** Put an old toy in.
> Take a new toy out.
> Put and take.
> Put and take."

After all of the boys had played 'Let's Trade,' Bill asked, "Can we play this new game the next time we come here?"

"No," said Steve. "The next time we play 'Let's Trade' will be when you all have old toys to trade. But I got my wish today. I have all new toys to play with."

The Birthday Party

"Soon it will be Jan's birthday," said Mother.

"Yes, I know," said Father. "Will we have a birthday party for her this time?"

"Yes," said Mother. "I will call all of her best friends to invite them to her birthday party."

"Are you going to make a birthday cake for them?" asked Father.

"Yes," said Mother. "I will make a birthday cake for Jan and all of her best friends. I know they will like that."

"I will help you make the cake," said Father.

"Thank you," said Mother. "We will all have a fun time at the party."

Soon, the day of Jan's birthday came. When she got out of bed, she said, "At last it is my birthday! I am happy today!

My mom will linvite all of my best friends to come here to our home for my birthday party. I know that they will be here on time. I will put on my best 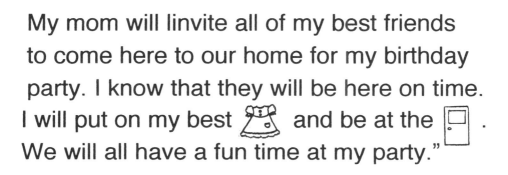 and be at the . We will all have a fun time at my party."

After a while, Jan's best friend, Beth, came to her house.

"Hello, Jan," said Beth. "Happy birthday! How old are you today?"

"I am 7 today," said Jan.

"This box is for you," said Beth.

"Oh, thank you, thank you," said Jan. "I know I will like it. I will put it right here on the ."

After a while, Pam and
Meg came to the house.

"Hello, Jan," they said. "Happy birthday!"

"This box is for you, Jan," said Meg.

"This box is for you, too," said Pam.

"Thank you, thank you!" said Jan.
"You are my good friends. I know I will like what you got for me. I will put this box and that box right here on the 🪑."

Then Steve and Pete got there. "Hello, Jan," they said. "Happy birthday! Look what we have for you. We know you will like it."

"Thank you, thank you!" said Jan. "I will put them right here on the 🪑."

Then Mother came in and said, "Now that you are all here, you can start to play a game."

After they had played the game for a while, Mother came by and said, "Now come in this room. It is time to have birthday cake."

They all ran to to the room.

While they all said together,

"Happy birthday to you,
Happy birthday to you,
Happy birthday to Jan,
Happy birthday to you,"

 . . . a dog came in the room.

"Oh, oh," said Pete. "That is my dog. I will tell him to go home. You did not invite him to this birthday party." He said, "Go home!"

The dog went out of the house. But he came back in the house when they did not look and got under the 🪑.

Soon, Mother came in the room with the cake. She said, "You will all like this cake, but do not take too much. Too much cake is not good for you. Take just a little."

"We know," they said. "We will take just a little."

While they ate the cake, Beth saw the dog under the 🪑. He wanted cake. She put a little cake under the 🪑 for him. The dog ate it all up.

Soon, Steve saw the dog under the 🪑. He put a little cake under the 🪑 for him. The dog ate it up.

After a while, Pam saw
the dog under the
She put a little cake under
the  for him. The dog
ate it all up.

 Then Pete and Meg saw
the dog and they put a
little cake under the
for him, too. The dog ate
it all up.

When Mother came back in the room
and saw that there was no cake there,
she said, "Where did all that cake go?
Did I tell you that too much cake is not
good for you?"

"Yes, that is right," they all said.

"But it is not we who
ate too much cake.
Just look under the
and see who ate too
much cake."

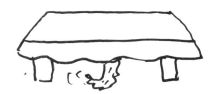

A Dog Can Help

When Pete got on his bike, he said, "Oh, oh. My bike will not start. I have to find out why."

He got off his bike and looked at it, up and down. After a while, he said, "There it is! Now I know why my bike will not start. It has a flat tire. I will ask my mother if I can walk my bike to the bike store to buy a new tire for my bike."

"Mom," said Pete. "Just look at this flat tire. My bike will not start. May I walk it to the bike store and get a new tire for it?"

"Oh, my!" said his mother. "How did you get a flat tire?"

"I do not know," said Pete. "But I do know that I will have to get a new tire soon. May I take it to the bike store now?"

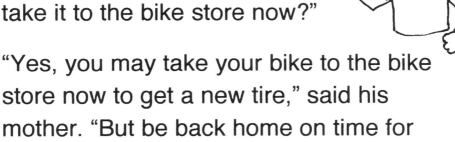

"Yes, you may take your bike to the bike store now to get a new tire," said his mother. "But be back home on time for dinner. Do not be late."

"All right," said Pete. "I will not forget to be back home on time for dinner. I will not be late."

And away he went to the bike store to get a new tire for his bike.

While Pete was at the bike store, he looked at this and he looked at that. It was fun to be at the bike store.

But what did he forget?

Yes! It was time for dinner and he was not back home right on time. He was late.

Father came home. He did not see Pete.
"Where is Pete?" he asked.
"Is he in his room?"

"No, he is not in his room," said Mother. "He went to the bike store to buy a new tire for his bike. He had a flat tire. I did tell him to get back here right on time for dinner. I do not know why he is late."

"I know what it is like to have fun at the bike store," said Father. "It can make you forget to go home on time."

After a while, Father said, "I know what we can do! We can send the dog to get Pete.

I will put a note on the dog and tell him to go and get Pete."

"That will be good if the dog can do it," said Mother. "I do not know if he can."

"I know he can do it," said Father. "Come here, Boy."

Father put a note on the dog and said to him, "Take this note to Pete. He is at the bike store. You know where that is. You go there with him all the time. Now run fast to the bike store with this note.

Go, Boy, go! Go, go, go!"

The dog looked at Mother.
The dog looked at Father.
He said, "Bow-wow! Bow-wow!"

Then away he ran. Away, away, away!

When the dog got to the bike store, he saw Pete. "Bow-wow! Bow-wow!"
he said.

Pete said, "What is that sound?"
Then he saw his dog.

"Just look at that," Pete said to the man at the bike store. "There is my dog with a note on his fur." The note said:

"Oh, oh!" said Pete to his dog. "Today I said to Mom, "I will not be late for dinner. I will not forget to get home on time. You came here to let me know that I was late. Good dog! Thank you, thank you! The next time, I will not forget.

Now I will give you a ride home."

And away they went.

Look Who is Big Now!

"Where is Bobby?" asked Father.

"I do not know," said Mother.
"Maybe he is in his room. I saw him in his room the last time I looked in there.
But I did tell him that he may go out of the house and play in the back yard."

"Thank you," said Father. "I will go out to the back yard and call him."

Away Father went to the back yard. He looked this way and that way. But Bobby was not out there in the back yard.

"I know that he likes to play with his new toys," said Mother. "Maybe he is in the play room."

Away Father went to look in the play room. But Bobby was not there.

After a while, Father said, "You know what Bobby is like. He must be up to something new."

"Yes, I know what Bobby is like," said Mother. "What can it be this time?"

"I do not know," said Father. But we will soon find out. Did you tell him that you made a cake for him for dinner?"

"Yes, I did," said Mother. "He will be back soon. He will be back in time for dinner."

And where was Bobby?

He was in his bedroom.

He said to himself, "I am big now. I know how to dress myself. I do not want my mother to help me dress. I can do it all by myself. And I know how to do it right." He looked in his big  and said,

"I see something red that I like.
I will put it on.

I see something new that I like.
I will put it on.

I see something old that I like.
I will put it on, too.

This is fun! I can dress myself!"

"Wow! Just look at me! I am done now! My mother and father will be happy to see me. They will know that I am a big boy. They will know that I can dress myself the next time, too! Look who is big now!"

When Mother saw Bobby, she said, "Oh, my! Just look at my big boy try to dress himself."

Father said, "Bobby, you did try to dress yourself. You did try to do a good job. But for a while, I want Mother to dress you. She will let you know when you can try to do it yourself. Do not forget it."

Take a good look at Bobby and you will know why Father said that.

One, Two, Three - GO!

"All of my friends have a bike," said Pam. "I wish I had a bike, too." On the way to the store, she saw something:

"Wow!" she said. "If I can win that race, I can buy a new bike for myself.

I will call my friend, Anna, and invite her to come to the race with me.

Maybe she will help me get in good shape for the race."

Hello, Anna,
   I want to invite you to come with me to a big race. I want to win the prize. Will you help me get in shape for the race?

Hello, Pam,
   Yes, I like to help you. I will be there right away! Good-by.

Soon they met in Pam's back yard.

Anna said, "This is how I will help you get in good shape for the race. When I say, 'One, two, three - Go,' I want you to run from this end of the yard to that end of the yard. Try to run fast.

One, two, three - GO!"

Pam ran from this end of the yard to that end of the yard.

The next day, they met at the same time in Pam's back yard. Anna said,

"One, two, three - GO!
You can do it!
You can do it!
Go, go, GO!"

Pam ran from this end of the yard to that end of the yard. She was fast.

They met at the same time the next day and the next day after that. Anna said,

"One, two, three - GO!
You can do it!
You can do it!
Go, go, GO!"

Pam was in good shape now. She said, "Anna, do you know what the best thing is?"

"No," said Anna. "What is the best thing?"

"The best thing is to win the prize," said Pam.

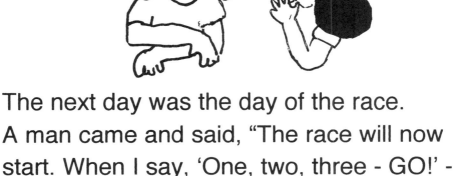

The next day was the day of the race. A man came and said, "The race will now start. When I say, 'One, two, three - GO!' - I want all of you to start to run.

One, two, three - GO!"

The three girls and the three boys started to run! Pam was fast. She ran past the three boys and the two girls. She wanted to win that prize to buy a new bike for herself.

But - oh, oh! There was something on the ground. Pam did not see it. Down she went - flat on the ground.

The three boys and the two girls ran past her.

"Oh, no!" said Pam.
"How can I win this race now?"

When Anna saw Pam flat down on the ground, she said, "Get up and run, Pam.

One, two, three - GO!
You can do it!
You can do it!
Go, go, GO!"

Then Pam said to herself, "Yes, I can try to do it. I can get up and try to win this race. I must win this race to get the prize."

Pam made herself get up and she started to run - fast, fast, fast. She was in good shape. She went past the three boys. She went past the two girls.

All the while, Anna said,

> "One, two, three - GO!
> You can do it!
> You can do it!
> GO, GO, go!"

Pam got to the end of the race. She looked back and saw the three boys and the two girls way back there.

The man said to Pam,

> "You WIN!
> The prize is for YOU!"

"Oh, Pam," said Anna.
"Good for you. You are the best!
Now you can buy yourself a new bike!"

"But it was you that made me win, Anna," said Pam. "Do you know what the best thing is?"

"Yes," said Anna.
"The best thing is to win the prize."

"No," said Pam. "The best thing is to have a friend like you!"

Just Do It!

"I wish I had my homework done," said Jan. "I just don't want to do it right now. I want to play with my cat. Which will I do now?"

"Why don't you ask Nell and Dell what to do?" said Beth. "They talk funny, but maybe they can help. See them there? I will call them."

"Hello, Nell and Dell," said Jan. "I don't want to do my homework right now. I want to play with my cat. Which will I do now?"

Nell said, "Do your homework right now.

> I would,
> if I could,
> and I think you should."

Dell said, "Do your homework right now.

> I think you should do it.
> That's all there is to it."

Then they said together,

> "So-o-o-o - JUST DO IT!"

Soon, Beth said to Jan, "I wish I had made my bed. I just don't want to do it right now. I want to ride my bike. Which will I do now?"

"Ask Nell and Dell what to do," said Jan. "They talk funny, but maybe they can help. There they are in the yard."

"Hello, Nell and Dell," said Beth. "I don't want to make my bed right now. I want to ride my bike. Which will I do now?"

Nell said, "Make your bed right now.

> I would,
> if I could,
> and I think you should."

Dell said, "Make your bed right now.

> I think you should do it.
> That's all there is to it."

Then they said together,

> "So-o-o-o - JUST DO IT!"

After a while, Pete saw Nell and Dell walk by his house. He said to himself, "I know it is time to walk my dog, but I just don't want to do it right now. I want to look at my fish swim. I think I will ask them which to do now. I know they talk funny, but maybe they can help me."

"Hello, Nell and Dell," said Pete. "I know it is time to walk my dog, but I just don't want to do it right now. I want to look at my fish swim. Which will I do now?"

Nell said, "Walk your dog right now.

> I would,
> if I could,
> and I think you should."

Dell said, "Walk your dog right now.

> I think you should do it.
> That's all there is to it."

Then they said together,

"So-o-o-o - JUST DO IT!"

Soon, Jan came by and saw Nell and Dell. She said, "I did what you said. I did my homework. Then I went out to play with my cat."

After a while, Beth came by and saw Nell and Dell. She said, "I did what you said. I made my bed. Then I went for a ride on my bike."

Then Pete came by and saw Nell and Dell. He said, "I did what you said. I walked my dog. Then I went to look at my fish swim."

Nell looked at Dell. Dell looked at Nell.

Then they said together -

"HOW COOL IS THAT?"

A New Pet

Mom, you said you would buy me a new pet if I did a good job on my homework. My homework is all done. Do you think it is a good job?

Oh, yes, Billy! I think you have done a good job on your homework. I did say I would buy you a new pet if it was done right.

Oh, boy! Could we get in the car now and go to the pet store?

Yes, Billy, but you have to know that a pet is not a toy. A pet is a big responsibility.

Why is that, Mom?

"I will tell you why a pet is a big responsibility.

You have to wash it.
You have to brush it.
You have to give it food right on time."

"I could do that for my new pet, Mom."

Soon, Billy and his mother got to the pet store.

They saw a little dog that said, "Bow-wow!"

They saw a little duck that said, "Quack, quack."

They saw a little cat that said, "Meow."

"Do you see something you would like to take home to live with you, Billy?"

The store man got the white rabbit from way up high and gave it to Billy.

"I will buy this white rabbit for you, Billy, if you don't forget that a rabbit is not a toy."

"Mom, I know that a rabbit is not a toy. A pet is a big responsibility.

I should wash it.
I should brush it.
I should give it
food right on time."

"That's right, Billy.

And you should know, too, that you have to give it love -

lots and lots of LOVE!"

Something Different

"Mom, I want to do something different today," said Jan. "I like to play in the yard, but not all the time. I want to do something different."

"Would you like to go to the playground?" asked Mother. "We could take our lunch there. That would be something different."

"Oh, yes!" said Jan. "I would love to go to the playground. That would be something different and it would be fun too!"

"Good," said Mother. "Let's go!"

"May I invite my best friend, Beth, to come to the playground with us?" asked Jan.

"Yes, you may invite your friend, Beth, to come with us," said Mother. "Tell her that we will take our lunch with us and we will come by her house with the car to get her soon."

Beth did say that she would like to go to the playground with them. So after a while, off they all went to the playground.

When they got to the playground, Jan said, "Look at that slide there, Beth. It's so much fun to go way up high in the sky on the slide and then slide back down."

"Yes," said Beth. "Let's race to the slide. There is a good sight of the playground from way up high."

After the slide ride, Beth said, "Would you like to take a ride on the seesaw?"

"Yes, I would," said Jan. "It's fun to sit on the seesaw and go way up high and then way back down to the ground. Up and down. Up and down. What fun! Let's go!"

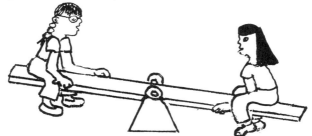

While Jan and Beth had fun on the seesaw, Mother got the lunch out of the car and put it under a 🌳. She said to herself, "I will call the girls when it is time for lunch." Then she went back to the car to cut some cake for lunch.

While Mother was at the car, a little squirrel came by and saw the lunch under the 🌳.

Oh, oh! There went the lunch!

When Mother came back from the car, she said, "Come here now, girls. Let's have lunch. The lunch is under the 🌳."

They all ran to the 🌳 - but there was no lunch there.

"Oh, my!" said Mother. "Where is our lunch? Where could it be?"

They looked here and they looked there. But there was no lunch to be found. So Mother said, "Play in the playground for a while and then we will have to go home for lunch."

Soon after that, Jan and Beth got on a swing and went high up in the sky. From up high, Jan could see the squirrel with the lunch.

111

"Look!" said Jan. "Do you see that squirrel out there? He has our lunch."

"Yes!" said Beth. "Let's go after it."

They got off the swing and started to run after the squirrel.

The squirrel saw them come after it so it ran out of the playground. Jan said, "Look! The squirrel ran that way."

And they ran after it.

The squirrel ran fast with the lunch. Jan and Beth ran fast, too. But they could not get the squirrel. The squirrel was too fast for them. Soon, the squirrel was out of sight.

"Oh, no!" said Beth. "We lost him."

"And we lost our lunch, too," said Jan.

After they looked here and they looked there, they said together, "That's not all that's lost. WE are lost, too!

Where are we?
What are we going to do now?"

"Let's ask that man at the bus stop how to get back to the playground," said Jan.

"I don't think we should talk to a man we don't know," said Beth.

"This is different," said Jan.
That man is a traffic cop.
He is there to help us. I
I will go and tell him that
we are lost."

When the traffic cop found out how they got lost, he said, "You should know that it is not good to go out of the playground without your mother. She must be looking for you."

"We know that we should not have done that," said Jan and Beth to the traffic cop.

"The squirrel is out of sight now," said the traffic cop, "so let's all go back to the playground together. Your mother will be happy to see you."

At the end of the day when Jan was on her way to bed, her mother said, "Jan, you wanted to do something different today. Was it fun?"

Jan said, "Mom, I wanted to do something different - but not THAT different!"

It's Show Time!

"Hi, Nell and Dell," said Bill. "Did you know that Miss White is going to let some children put on a show for us?"

Tell me when and where, and I will see you there.

"The show will be at school on the last day of school," said Bill.

A show at school? That's cool!"

"Which children do you think will be in the show?" asked Bill.

Which children are in the show? That is something I do not know.

"The children in the show are Pete and Jan and Tom and Beth," said Bill.

That will be much fun. Now we have to run.

"Good-by," said Bill. "See you at the show!"

Soon it was the last day of school. Miss White walked in the room and said, "All of you children sit back now and have fun.

It's show time!!!"

Pete came in with a big box. He got Puppet One out of the box. It said, "Bow-wow. Where is my food?"

"Wow!" said Bill. "He can sound just like a dog."

Pete got Puppet Two out of the box. It said, "Meow, I don't want that dog to get me."

This is something new.

He can sound like a cat, too.

Pete got Puppet Three out of the box. It said, "Quack, quack. I can swim on my back"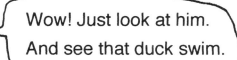

Wow! Just look at him.
And see that duck swim.

Then Pete made a big bow and went out of the room. The children started to clap and clap. Miss White said, "I can see that you children love a show."

Next, Jan came in. You can see what she did in the show.

Then she made a big bow and went out of the room. The children started to clap and clap.

After that, Tom came in and did his thing. See it go round and round.

Look at him go! What a show!

On the way out of the room, Tom said to Nell and Dell, "What did you think of that?" They said together:

You **rock!**

Last of all, Beth came in and said, "I am going to sing for you."

She could sing so good that the children started to clap and clap.

Then Beth made a big bow and went out of the room.

And that was the end of the show.

When the show was done, one of the children who was in the show asked Miss White, "How did you like the show? What do you think of us?"

Miss White said, "Just look at the word I am going to put up here. If you know the word, don't say it. I can tell if you know it by your smile. I want to give you all time to think."

After all the children had time to think, Miss White said, "This is what I think all of you are.

Now, who can tell me what the word is?"

They all said together:

FANTASTIC!!!

Primer

PART I

Vocabulary Word List

Pages 1 - 4

p. 1 - stop
      Bobby
      Mom
      walk *
p. 2 - fast
p. 3 - red

Pages 5 - 8

p. 5 - Dad
      slow
      must
      ask
      talk
p. 6 - them
p. 8 - look<u>ing</u>

Pages 9 - 12

p. 9 - lost
      Bob
      Pat
      find
      cut
      out **
p. 10 - Good
p. 11 - Bobby<u>'s</u>

Pages 13 - 16

p. 13 - What
       ask<u>ed</u>
       found ***
       No
p. 14 - give
       Baby
p. 15 - his
p. 16 - if
       say

Pages 17 - 20

p. 17 - ran
       back
       when
p. 18 - why
       toy
p 19 - toy<u>s</u>
       which
p. 20 - then

Pages 21 - 24

p. 21 - be
       live
       yes
       how
p. 22 - was
       sit
       stand
p. 23 - look<u>ed</u>
p. 24 - let

Pages 25 - 28

p. 25 - spell
       word
       Tom
       Jan
       Bill
p. 26 - best
       spell<u>er</u>
       who
p. 27 - sound
p. 28 - word<u>s</u>

Pages 29 - 33

p. 29 - go<u>ing</u>
       Park
       There
       our
       bus
       start
p. 30 - where
       went
       much

Pages 34 - 38

p. 34 - Scout
       Bow-wow
p. 35 - way
p. 36 - man
       by
       wish
       Good-by
       had
p. 37 - got
p. 38 - want<u>ed</u>
       call

Page 39 - 43

p. 39 - clay
       hand
p. 41 - house
       famiily
p. 42 - But
p. 43 - into
       of

Pages 44 - 48

p. 44 - happy
       walk<u>ing</u>
       doll
       duck
       Hello
       quack
p. 45 - truck
       frog
       jump<u>ed</u>
p. 46 - met
p. 47 - best

Pages 49 - 54

p. 49 - saw ****
       box
       friend
       work
       day
       today
p. 51 - boy<u>s</u>
       Beth
       may
       your
p. 53   girl<u>s</u>

* Introduce the "**alk**" Sight Family beforehand.
** Introduce the "**ou**" Sight Family beforehand.
*** Introduce the "**ound**" Sight Family beforehand.
**** Introduce the "**aw**" Sight Family beforehand.

Word-for-Word Dialogue
Primer
PART I

Now that you have completed Pre-Primer I, Pe-Primer II, and Pre-Primer III, begin to introduce the **Consonant Blends**, as detailed in *At Last!* beginning on p. 141. It is also time to begin to introduce the **Short Vowel Families**, as detailed in *At Last!* beginning on p. 145.

We will also be developing word endings, **s**, **ed**, **ing**, **'s**, **er**, and **Compound Words**.

Now, you are ready to begin the Primer!

> 1. Write a list of the words to be introduced that day for the assigned pages, as illustrated on p. 99-101 in *At Last!*.
> 2. Introduce the words as scripted below.

Following is the word-for-word dialogue between teacher and student for introducing every word in this reader:

Pages 1 - 4

NOTE: Introduce the Sight Family "**alk**" <u>during</u> <u>the</u> <u>Phonics</u> <u>Period</u> before introducing the word "walk."

	Teacher:	**Student:**
stop -	Underline O-P.	<u>o p</u>
	What's the family?	o p
	What's the word?	s t o p
Bobby -	Underline O-B.	<u>o b</u>
	What's the family?	o b
	Add "B."	B o b
	KEEP GOING - What's the word?	B o b b y
	Yes, "Y" on the <u>end</u> says "E."	
Mom -	Underline O-M.	<u>o m</u>
	What's the family?	o m
	What's the word?	M o m
walk -	Underline A-L-K.	<u>a l k</u>
	What's the Sight Family?	a l k
	What's the word?	w a l k
fast -	Underline A-S-T.	<u>a s t</u>
	What's the family?	a s t
	What's the word?	f a s t
red -	Underline E-D.	<u>e d</u>
	What's the family?	e d
	What's the word?	r e d

Pages 5 - 8

	Teacher:	**Student:**
Dad -	Underline A-D.	<u>a d</u>
	What's the family?	a d
	What's the word?	D a d
slow -	If you're not fast, you might be -	s l o w
	What's the clue?	s<u>l o w</u>
must -	Underline U-S-T.	<u>u s t</u>
	What's the family?	u s t
	What's the word?	m u s t
ask -	Underline A-S-K.	<u>a s k</u>
	What's the family?	a s k
	What's the word?	a s k
talk -	Underline A-L-K.	<u>a l k</u>
	What's the Sight Family?	a l k
	What's the word?	t a l k
them -	Underline E-M.	<u>e m</u>
	What's the family?	e m
	What's the word?	t h e m
look -	We had this word. Can you read it?	l o o k
looking -	What's the next word?	l o o k i n g
	Underline "ing."	l o o k<u>i n g</u>

Pages 9 - 12

NOTE: Introduce the Sight Family "**ou**" <u>during the Phonic Period</u> before introducing the word "out."

lost -	Underline O-S-T.	<u>o s t</u>
	What's the family?	o s t
	What's the word?	l o s t
Bob -	Underline O-B.	<u>o b</u>
	What's the family?	o b
	What's the word?	B o b
Pat -	Underline A-T.	<u>a t</u>
	What's the family?	a t
	What's the word?	P a t
find -	If you lost something, you would want to -	f i n d
	What's the clue?	f<u>i n d</u>
cut -	Underline U-T.	<u>u t</u>
	What's the family?	u t
	What's the word?	c u t
out -	Underline O-U.	<u>o u</u>
	What's the Sight Family?	o u
	KEEP GOING - What's the word?	o u t
Good -	That really looks -	G o o d
	What's the clue?	<u>G</u>o o <u>d</u>

Pages 9 - 12 (Cont'd.)

	Teacher:	**Student:**
Bobby -	We had this word. Can you read it?	B o b b y
Bobby's -	When something belongs to someone, we add **'s**.	
	Underline the **'s**. (It's called "possessive.")	B o b b y <u>'s</u>
	What's the word?	B o b b y 's

Pages 13 - 16

NOTE: Introduce the Sight Family "**ound**" <u>during</u> <u>the</u> <u>Phonic</u> <u>Period</u> before introducing the word "found."

What -	This word is "what," as in "<u>What</u> did you find?"	
	What's the clue?	W <u>h a</u> t
ask -	We had this word. Can you read it?	a s k
asked -	What's the next word?	a s k e d
	Underline "ed."	a s k <u>e d</u>
	(**Note**: Offer any explanation needed.)	
found -	Underline O-U-N-D.	<u>o u n d</u>
	What's the Sight Family?	o u n d
	What's the word?	f o u n d
No -	The answer to the question is -	N o
	What's the clue?	<u>N</u> o
give -	How much money can you -	g i v e
	What's the clue?	g <u>i v</u> e
Baby -	Look at that cute little -	B a b y
	What's the clue?	B <u>a b y</u>
	Yes, "Y" on the <u>end</u> says "E."	
his -	Underline I-S.	i <u>s</u>
	What's the family?	i s
	What's the word?	h i s
	(**Note:** Exaggerate the sound of "s" to assist decoding.)	
if -	Underline I-F.	<u>i f</u>
	What's the family?	i f
	What's the word	i f
say -	Underline A-Y.	<u>a y</u>
	What's the Sight Family?	a y
	What's the word?	s a y

Pages 17 - 20

ran -	Underline A-N.	<u>a n</u>
	What's the family?	a n
	What's the word?	r a n
back -	Underline A-C-K.	<u>a c k</u>
	What's the family?	a c k
	What's the word?	b a c k

Pages 17 - 20 (Cont'd.)

	Teacher:	**Student:**
when -	Underline E-N.	<u>e n</u>
	What's the family?	e n
	What's the word?	w h e n
why -	He has gone home and I don't know -	w h y
	What's the clue?	w <u>h y</u>
	Yes, "Y" on the <u>end</u> says "I."	
toy -	Underline O-Y.	<u>o y</u>
	What's the Sight Family?	o y
	What's the word?	t o y
toys -	What's the next word?	t o y s
	Underline "s."	t o y <u>s</u>
which -	Underline I-C-H.	<u>i c h</u>
	What's the family?	i c h
	What's the word?	w h i c h
then -	Underline E-N.	<u>e n</u>
	What's the family	e n
	What's the word?	t h e n

Pages 21 - 24

be -	Someone is at the door. Who can it -	b e
	What's the clue?	b <u>e</u>
live -	I see a house. Is that where you -	l i v e
	What's the clue?	l <u>i</u> <u>v</u> e
yes -	Underline E-S.	<u>e s</u>
	What's the family?	e s
	What's the word?	y e s
how -	Underline O-W.	<u>o w</u>
	What's the Sight Family?	o w
	What's the word	h o w
was -	Someone was here but I don't know who it -	w a s
	What's the clue?	<u>w</u> a <u>s</u>
	(**Note:** Exaggerate the sound of "s" to assist decoding.)	
sit -	Underline I-T.	<u>i t</u>
	What's the family?	i t
	What's the word?	s i t
stand -	Underline A-N-D.	<u>a n d</u>
	What's the family?	a n d
	What's the word?	s t a n d
look -	We had this word. Can you read it?	l o o k
looked -	What's the next word?	l o o k e d
	Underline "ed."	l o o k <u>e d</u>
let -	Underline E-T.	<u>e t</u>
	What's the family?	e t
	What's the word?	l e t

Pages 25 - 28

spell -	Underline E-L-L.	<u>ell</u>
	What's the family?	e l l
	What's the word?	s p e l l
speller -	What's the next word?	s p e l l e r
	Underline "er."	s p e l l <u>e r</u>
word -	Can you read this -	w o r d
	What's the clue?	w<u>o</u>r d
words -	What's the next word?	w o r d s
	Underline "s."	w o r d <u>s</u>
Tom -	Underline O-M.	<u>o m</u>
	What's the family?	o m
	What's the word?	T o m
Jan -	Underline A-N.	<u>a n</u>
	What's the family?	a n
	What's the word?	J a n
Bill -	Underline I-L-L.	<u>i l l</u>
	What's the family?	i l l
	What's the word?	B i l l
best -	Underline E-S-T.	<u>e s t</u>
	What's the family?	e s t
	What's the word?	b e s t
who -	This word is "who," as in "<u>Who</u> is at the door?"	
	What's the clue?	w <u>h</u> o
sound -	Underline O-U-N-D.	<u>o u n d</u>
	What's the Sight Family?	o u n d
	What's the word?	s o u n d

Pages 29 - 33

go -	We had this word. Can you read it?	g o
going -	What's the next word?	g o i n g
	Underling "ing.."	g o <u>i n g</u>
Park -	It's fun to play in the -	P a r k
	What's the clue?	P <u>a r</u> k
There -	Look way over -	T h e r e
	What's the clue?	T h <u>e r</u> e
our -	This word is "our," as in "This is <u>our</u> class."	
	What's the clue?	o <u>u</u> r
bus -	Underline U-S.	<u>u s</u>
	What's the family?	u s
	What's the word?	b u s
start -	This word is "start," as in "The bus will <u>start</u>."	
	What's the clue?	s t <u>a</u> r t
where -	This word is "where," as in "Where is the bus?"	
	What's the clue?	w h <u>e r</u> e

Pages 29 - 33 (Cont'd.)

went -	Underline E-N-T.	<u>e n</u> t
	What's the family?	e n t
	What's the word?	w e n t
much -	Underline U-C-H.	**<u>u c h</u>**
	What's the family?	u c h
	What's the word?	m u c h

Pages 34 - 38

Scout -	I see a Girl Scout and a Boy -	S c o u t
	What's the clue?	<u>S c o u t</u>
Bow-wow -	Underline O-W and O-W.	B <u>o w</u> - w <u>o w</u>
	What's the Sight Family?	o w
	What's the word?	B o w - w o w
way -	Underline A-Y.	**<u>a y</u>**
	What's the Sight Family?	a y
	What's the word?	w a y
man -	Underline A-N.	**<u>a n</u>**
	What's the family?	a n
	What's the word?	m a n
by -	This word is "by," as in "A man went <u>by</u>."	
	What 's the clue?	b y
	Yes, "Y" on the <u>end</u> says "I."	
wish -	Underline I-S-H.	**<u>i s h</u>**
	What's the family?	i s h
	What;s the word.	w i s h
Good -	We had this word. Can you read it?	G o o d
by -	We had this word. Can you read it?	b y
Good-by -	What's the next word?	G o o d - b y
had -	Underline A-D.	**<u>a d</u>**
	What's the family?	a d
	What's the word?	h a d
got -	Underline O-T.	**<u>o t</u>**
	What's the family?	o t
	What's the word?	g o t
want -	We had this word. Can you read it?	w a n t
wanted -	What's the next word?	w a n t e d
	Underline "ed."	w a n t <u>e d</u>
call -	Underline A-L-L.	**<u>a l l</u>**
	What's the Sight Family?	a l l
	What's the word?	c a l l

Pages 39 - 43

clay -	Underline A-Y.	**<u>a y</u>**
	What's the Sight Family?	a y
	What's the word?	c l a y

Pages 39 - 43 (Cont'd.)

hand -	Underline A-N-D.	**a n d**
	What's the family?	a n d
	What's the word?	h a n d
house -	You live in a -	h o u s e
	What's the clue?	h <u>o u s</u> e
But -	Underline U-T.	**u t**
	What's the family?	u t
	What's the word?	b u t
family -	Underline A-M.	**a m**
	What's the family?	a m
	Add "f."	f a m
	Underline I-L.	**i l**
	What's the family?	i l
	GO BACK -	f a m i l
	KEEP GOING - What's the word?	f a m i l y
in -	We had this word. Can you read it?	i n
to -	We had this word. Can you read it?	t o
into -	What's the next word?	i n t o
	Yes. When you put two words together, it's called a "**Compound**" word.	
of -	This word is "of," as in "He came out <u>of</u> the house."	
	What's the clue?	o f
	(**Note:** You can exaggerate the sound of "f" to assist decoding.)	

Pages 44 - 48

happy -	Underline A-P.	**a p**
	What's the family?	a p
	Add "h."	h a p
	KEEP GOING - What's the word?	h a p p y
walk -	Underline A-L-K.	**a l k**
	What's the Sight Family?	a l k
	What's the word?	w a l k
walking -	What's the next word?	w a l k i n g
	Underline "ing."	w a l k <u>i n g</u>
doll -	Underline O-L-L.	**o l l**
	What's the family?	o l l
	What's the word?	d o l l
duck -	Underline U-C-K.	**u c k**
	What's the family?	u c k
	What's the word"	d u c k
Hello -	Underline E-L-L.	**e l l**
	What's the family?	e l l
	Add "h."	h e l l
	KEEP GOING - What's the word?	h e l l o
quack -	Underline A-C-K.	**a c k**
	What's the family?	a c k
	What's the word?	q u a c k

Pages 44 - 48 (Cont'd.)

truck -	Underline U-C-K.	<u>u c k</u>
	What's the family?	u c k
	What's the word?	t r u c k
frog -	Underline O-G.	<u>o g</u>
	What's the family?	o g
	What's the word?	f r o g
jump -	We had this word. Can you read it?	j u m p
	What's the next word?	j u m p e d
jumped -	Underline "ed."	j u m p <u>e d</u>
met -	Underline E-T.	<u>e t</u>
	What's the family?	e t
	What's the word?	m e t
best -	Underline E-S-T.	<u>e s t</u>
	What's the family?	e s t
	What's the word?	b e s t

Pages 49 - 54

NOTE: Introduce the Sight Family "**aw**" <u>during</u> <u>the</u> <u>Phonic</u> <u>Period</u> before introducing the word "saw."

saw -	Underline A-W/	<u>a w</u>
	What's the Sight Family?	a w
	What's the word?	s a w
box -	Underline O-X.	<u>o x</u>
	What's the family?	o x
	What's the word?	b o x
friend -	You are my best -	f r i e n d
	What's the clue?	f <u>r i e n d</u>
work -	Sometimes we play and sometimes we -	w o r k
	What's the clue?	<u>w</u> o <u>r</u> k
to -	We ha d this word. Can you read it?	t o
day -	Underline A-Y.	<u>a y</u>
	What's the Sight Family?	a y
	What's the word?	d a y
today -	What's the compound word?	t o d a y
boy -	We had this word. Can you read it?	b o y
boys -	What's the next word?	b o y s
	Underline "s."	b o y <u>s</u>
Beth -	Underline E-T-H.	<u>e t h</u>
	What's the family?	e t h
	What's the word?	B e t h
may -	Underline A-Y.	<u>a y</u>
	What's the Sight Family?	a y
	What's the word?	m a y
your -	This word is "your," as in "This is <u>your</u> play house."	
	What's the clue?	<u>y</u> o <u>u r</u>
girl -	We had this word. Can you read it?	g i r l
girls -	What's the next word?	g i r l s
	Underline "s."	g i r l <u>s</u>

Mid-Primer
PART II
Vocabulary Word List

Pages 57 - 60

p. 57 - fly
bird
Pete
bike
ride
time
nest
p. 58 - fall
p. 60 - next
sky

Pages 61 - 65

p. 61 - job
done
here
make
bed
know
together
p. 62 - Steve
while
p. 63 - start<u>ed</u>
came
p. 64 - forget

Pages 66 - 69

p, 66 - new *
game
name
rhyme
sentence
last
p. 67 - same
end
like
p. 69 - home

Pages 70 - 73

p. 70 - let'<u>s</u>
trade
room
old
play<u>ed</u>
after
take
put
friend<u>s</u>
p. 72 - an
right **

Pages 74 - 79

p, 74 - birthday
party
soon
invite
cake
they
thank
p. 77 - under
p. 78 - ate

Pages 80 - 85

p. 80 - has
flat
tire
store
buy
p. 81 - dinner
late
<u>a</u>way
p. 83 - send
note

131

Pages 86 - 89

p. 86 - maybe
yard
p. 87 - like<u>s</u>
some
thing
something
made
p. 88 - bedroom
himself
dress
myself
p. 89 - try
yourself

Pages 90 - 97

p. 90 - one
two
three
race
win
prize
shape
p. 91 - from
p. 94 - past
herself
ground

Pages 98 - 103

p. 98 - homework
don't
Nell
Dell
p. 99 - would
could
should
think
that'<u>s</u>
so
p. 103 - walk<u>ed</u>
cool

Pages 104 - 107

p. 104 - Billy
responsibility
p. 105 - wash
brush
food
meow
p. 106 - white
rabbit
high ***
p. 107 - lot
lots
love

Pages 108 - 114

p. 108 - different
playground
lunch
p. 109 - slide
it's
sight
p. 110 - seesaw
squirrel
p. 111 - swing
p. 113 - traffic
cop
p. 114 - without

Pages 115 - 120

p. 115 - show
Miss
children
school
p. 116 - puppet
p. 117 - clap
p. 118 - round
rock
p. 119 - sing
smile

* Introduce the "**ew**" Sight Family beforehand.
** Introduce the "**ight**" Sight Family beforehand.
*** Introduce "**igh**" Sight Family beforehand.

Word-for-Word Dialogue
Mid-Primer
PART II

Now that you have completed Part I of the Primer, begin to introduce the **Long Vowel Families (e-on-the end)**, as detailed in *At Last!* beginning on p. 181. We will also continue to develop word endings, possessives, and compound words, and begin to introduce **Contractions**.

Now, you are ready to begin the Mid-Primer!

> 1. Write a list of the words to be introduced that day for the assigned pages, as illustrated on p. 99-101 in *At Last!*.
> 2. Introduce the words as scripted below.

Following is the word-for-word dialogue between teacher and student for introducing every word in this reader:

<u>Pages 57 - 60</u>

	Teacher:	**Student:**
fly -	A bird can -	f l y
	What's the clue?	<u>f l y</u>
bird -	This word is "bird," as in "A <u>bird</u> can fly."	
	What's the clue?	b <u>ir</u> d
Pete -	Underline E-T-E.	<u>e t e</u>
	What's the family?	e t e
	What's the word?	P e t e
bike -	Underline I-K-E.	<u>i k e</u>
	What's the family?	i k e
	What's the word?	b i k e
ride -	Underline I-D-E.	<u>i d e</u>
	What's the family?	i d e
	What's the word?	r i d e
time -	Underline I-M-E.	<u>i m e</u>
	What's the family?	i m e
	What's the word?	t i m e
nest -	Underline E-S-T.	<u>e s t</u>
	What's the family?	e s t
	What's the word?	n e s t
fall -	Underline A-L-L.	<u>a l l</u>
	What's the sight family?	a l l
	What's the word?	f a l l

	Teacher:	**Student:**
next -	Underline E-X-T.	<u>ext</u>
	What's the family?	e x t
	What's the word?	n e x t
sky -	A bird can fly way up to the -	s k y
	What's the clue?	<u>sk</u> y

<u>Pages 61- 65</u>

job -	Underline O-B.	<u>o b</u>
	What's the family?	o b
	What's the word?	j o b
done -	I finished my work. It is all -	d o n e
	What's the clue?	<u>d</u> o <u>n</u> e
here -	Underline E-R-E.	<u>ere</u>
	What's the family?	e r e
	What's the word?	h e r e
make -	Underline A-K-E.	<u>a k e</u>
	What's the family?	a k e
	What's the word?	m a k e
bed -	Underline E-D.	<u>e d</u>
	What's the family?	e d
	What's the word?	b e d
know -	This word is "know," as in "I <u>know</u> your name."	
	What's the clue?	k <u>n o</u> w
to -	We had this word. Can you read it?	t o
together -	The next word is "together." What's the clue?	t o <u>g e t h ə r</u>
Steve -	Underline E-V-E.	<u>e v e</u>
	What's the family?	e v e
	What's the word?	S t e v e
while -	Underline I-L-E.	<u>i l e</u>
	What's the family?	i l e
	What's the word?	w h i l e
start -	We had this word. Can you read it?	s t a r t
started -	What's the next word?	s t a r t e d
	Underline "ed."	s t a r t <u>e d</u>
came -	Underline A-M-E.	<u>a m e</u>
	What's the family?	a m e
	What's the word?	c a m e
for get -	We had these two words. Can you read them?	f o r g e t
forget -	What's the Compound word?	f o r g e t

<u>Pages 66- 69</u>

NOTE: Introduce the Sight Family "**ew**" <u>during</u> <u>the</u> <u>Phonic</u> <u>Period</u> before introducing the word "new."

(**Note:** Rhyming words are not formally introduced. The children can decode these independently.)

	Teacher:	**Student:**
new -	Underline E-W.	<u>e w</u>
	What's the Sight Family?	e w
	What's the word?	n e w
game -	Underline A-M-E.	<u>a m e</u>
	What's the family?	a m e
	What's the word?	g a m e
name -	Underline A-M-E.	<u>a m e</u>
	What's the family?	a m e
	What's the word?	n a m e
rhyme -	This word is "rhyme," as in "It's fun to <u>rhyme</u> words."	
	What's the clue?	<u>r</u> h <u>y</u> m e
	(**Note:** To assist decoding, "y" says "i.")	
sentence -	You put a period at the end of a -	s e n t e n c e
	What's the clue?	<u>s</u> e n <u>t</u> e n <u>c</u> e
last -	Underline A-S-T.	<u>a s t</u>
	What's the family?	a s t
	What's the word?	f a s t
same -	Underline A-M-E.	<u>a m e</u>
	What's the family?	a m e
	What's the word?	s a m e
end -	Underline E-N-D.	<u>e n d</u>
	What's the family?	e n d
	What's the word?	e n d
like -	Underline I-K-E.	<u>i k e</u>
	What's the family?	i k e
	What's the word?	l i k e
home -	Underline O-M-E.	<u>o m e</u>
	What's the family?	o m e
	What the word?	h o m e

<u>Pages 70- 73</u>

NOTE: Introduce the Sight Family "**ight**" <u>during</u> <u>the</u> <u>P</u>honic <u>P</u>eriod before introducing the word "right."

let us -	We had these two words. Can you read them?	l e t u s
let's -	When two words are combined together and the last word is shortened, it is called a "contraction." In place of the missing letter is put an apostrophe.	
	What letter is missing?	u
	What's the contraction?	l e t ' s
trade -	Underline A-D-E.	<u>a d e</u>
	What's the family?	a d e
	What's the word?	t r a d e
room -	I sleep in my own bed -	r o o m
	What's the clue?	<u>r</u> <u>o o</u> m

135

	Teacher:	**Student:**
old -	If it's not new, it might be -	o l d
	What's the clue?	<u>o</u> l <u>d</u>
play -	We had this word. Can you read it?	p l a y
played -	What's the next word?	p l a y e d
	Underline "ed."	p l a y <u>e d</u>
after -	Underline A-F.	<u>**a f**</u>
	What's the family?	a f
	Underline E-R.	<u>**e r**</u>
	What's the sight family?	e r
	Add "t."	t e r
	What's the word?	a f t e r
take -	Underline A-K-E.	<u>**a k e**</u>
	What's the family?	a k e
	What's the word?	t a k e
put -	This word is "put," as in "Please <u>put</u> that here."	
	What's the clue?	<u>p</u> u <u>t</u>
friend -	We had this word. Can you read it?	f r i e n d
friends -	What's the next word?	f r i e n d s
	Underline "s."	f r i e n d <u>s</u>
an -	Underline A-N.	<u>**a n**</u>
	What's the family?	a n
	What's the word?	a n
right -	Underline I-G-H-T.	<u>**i g h t**</u>
	What's the sight family?	i g h t
	What's the word?	r i g h t

<u>Pages 74 - 79</u>

birth -	The day you are born is the day of your -	b i r t h
	What's the clue?	<u>b</u> i <u>r t h</u>
day -	We had this word. Can you read it?	d a y
birthday -	What's the compound word?	b i r t h d a y
party -	Will you come to my birthday -	p a r t y
	What's the clue?	<u>p</u> a <u>r t y</u>
soon -	We will meet again very -	s o o n
	What's the clue?	<u>s</u> <u>o o</u> <u>n</u>
invite -	Underline I-N.	<u>**i n**</u>
	What's the family?	i n
	Underline I-T-E.	<u>**i t e**</u>
	What's the family?	i t e
	Add "v."	v i t e
	What's the word?	i n v i t e
cake -	Underline A-K-E.	<u>**a k e**</u>
	What's the family?	a k e
	What's the word?	c a k e

	Teacher:	**Student:**
they -	This word is "they," as in "<u>They</u> are coming here."	
	What's the clue?	t<u>h</u>e y
thank -	Underline A-N-K.	<u>a n k</u>
	What's the family?	a n k
	What's the word?	t h a n k
under -	Underline U--N.	<u>u n</u>
	What's the family?	u n
	Underline E-R.	<u>e r</u>
	What's the family?	e r
	Add "d."	d e r
	What's the word?	u n d e r
ate -	Underline A-T-E.	<u>a t e</u>
	What's the family?	a t e
	What's the word?	a t e

Pages 80 - 85

has -	Do you know how many cookies he -	h a s
	What's the clue?	<u>h</u> a <u>s</u>
	(**Note:** Exaggerate the "s" sound to assist decoding.)	
flat -	Underline A-T.	<u>a t</u>
	What's the family?	a t
	What's the word?	f l a t
tire -	Underline I-R-E.	<u>i r e</u>
	What's the family?	i r e
	What's the word?	t i r e
store -	Underline O-R-E.	<u>o r e</u>
	What's the family?	o r e
	What's the word?	s t o r e
buy -	When you go to the store, what are you going to -	b u y
	What's the clue?	<u>b</u> u y
dinner -	Underline I-N.	<u>i n</u>
	What's the family	i n
	Underline E-R.	<u>e r</u>
	What's the family?	e r
	Add "n."	n e r
	What's the word?	d i n n e r
late -	Underline A-T-E.	<u>a t e</u>
	What's the family?	a t e
	What's the word?	l a t e
way -	We had this word. Can you read it?	w a y
away -	When you add "a," the word is "away."	a w a y
	Underline "a."	<u>a</u> w a y
	(**Note:** A long "a" sound assists decoding. With the constant repetition of these "a" words, children automatically revert to the correct pronunciation.)	

	Teacher:	**Student:**
send -	Underline E-N-D.	<u>e n d</u>
	What's the family?	e n d
	What's the word?	s e n d
note -	Underline O-T-E.	<u>o t e</u>
	What's the family?	o t e
	What's the word?	n o t e

Pages 86 - 89

	Teacher:	**Student:**
may be -	We had these words. Can you read them?	m a y b e
maybe -	What's the compound word?	m a y b e
yard -	I like to play in my back -	y a r d
	What's the clue?	<u>y a r d</u>
like -	We had this word. Can you read it?	l i k e
likes -	What's the next word?	l i k e s
	Underline "s."	l i k e <u>s</u>
some -	That looks good to eat. May I have -	s o m e
	What's the clue?	<u>s</u> <u>o</u> <u>m</u> e
thing -	Underline I-N-G.	<u>i n g</u>
	What's the family?	i n g
	What's the word?	t h i n g
something -	What's the compound word?	s o m e t h i n g
made -	Underline A-D-E.	<u>a d e</u>
	What's the family?	a d e
	What's the word?	m a d e
bed room -	We had these words. Can you read them?	b e d r o o m
bedroom -	What's the compound word?	b e d r o o m
him -	We had this word. Can you read it?	h i m
self -	Underline E-L-F.	<u>e l f</u>
	What's the family?	e l f
	What's the word?	s e l f
himself -	What;s the compound word?	h i m s e l f
dress -	Underline E-S-S.	<u>e s s</u>
	What's the family?	e s s
	What's the word?	d r e s s
my self -	We had these words. Can you read them?	m y s e f
myself -	What's the compound word?	m y s e l f
try -	You don't know if you can do it until you -	t r y
	What's the clue?	<u>t r y</u>
your self -	We had these words. Can you read them?	y o u r s e l f
yourself -	What's the compound word?	y o u r s e l f

Pages 90 - 97

	Teacher:	**Student:**
one -	This word is "one," as in "I have <u>one</u> ball." What's the clue? (**Note:** Configuration clue: The "o" looks like "one" ball.)	o <u>n</u> e
two -	This word is "two," as in "I have <u>two</u> balls." What's the clue?	<u>t</u> w o
three -	This number is "three," as in "I have <u>three</u> balls." What's the clue?	t h <u>r</u> e e
race -	Underline A-C-E. What's the family? What's the word?	**<u>a c e</u>** a c e r a c e
win -	Underline I-N. What's the family? What's the word?	**<u>i n</u>** i n w i n
prize -	Underline I-Z-E. What's the family? What's the word?	**<u>i z e</u>** i z e p r i z e
shape -	Underline A-P-E. What's the family? What's the word?	**<u>a p e</u>** a p e s h a p e
from -	Where did you come - What's the clue?	f r o m f<u>r</u> o m
past -	Underline A-S-T. What's the family? What's the word?	**<u>a s t</u>** a s t p a s t
her self - **herself** -	We had these words. Can you read them? What's the compound word?	h e r s e l f h e r s e l f
ground -	Underline O-U-N-D. What's the sight family? What's the word?	**<u>o u n d</u>** o u n d g r o u n d

Pages 98 - 103

home work - **homework** -	We had these words. Can you read them? What's the compound word?	h o m e w o r k h o m e w o r k
do not -	We had these two words. Can you read them?	d o n o t
don't -	When two words are combined together and the last word is shortened, it is called a "contraction." In place of the missing letter is put an apostrophe. What letter is missing? What's the contraction? (**Note:** Guide the pronunciation because this is an irregular contraction.)	o d o n ' t

139

	Teacher:	**Student:**
Nell -	Underline E-L-L.	<u>e l l</u>
	What's the family?	e l l
	What's the word?	N e l l
Dell -	Underline E-L-L.	<u>e l l</u>
	What's the family?	e l l
	What's the word?	D e l l
would -	This word is "would," as in "<u>Would</u> you please come here?"	
	What's the clue?	<u>w</u> o u l <u>d</u>
could -	This word is "could," as in "I <u>could</u> do that for you."	
	What's the clue?	<u>c</u> o u l <u>d</u>
should -	This word is "should," as in "I <u>should</u> do that now."	
	What's the clue?	<u>s</u> <u>h</u> o u l <u>d</u>
think -	Underline I-N-K.	<u>i n k</u>
	What's the family?	i n k
	What's the word?	t h i n k
that is -	We had these words. Can you read them?	t h a t i s
that's -	What's the contraction?	t h a t ' s
so -	This word is "so," as in "It was fun. <u>So</u> we did it."	
	What's the clue?	<u>s</u> o
walk -	We had this word. Can you read it?	<u>w a l k</u>
walked -	What's the next word?	w a l k e d
	Underline "ed."	w a l k <u>e d</u>
cool -	The weather is not warm. It is quite -	c o o l
	What's the clue?	<u>c</u> o o l

Pages 104 - 107

NOTE: Introduce the Sight Family "**Igh**" <u>during the</u> <u>Phonic</u> <u>Period</u> before introducing the word "high."

Bill -	We had this word. Can you read it?	B i l l
Billy -	What's the next word?	B i l l y
	Underline "y."	B i l l <u>y</u>
responsibility -	This word is "responsibility," as in " A pet is a big responsibility."	
	What's the clue?	<u>r e s p o n s i b i l i t y</u>
wash -	This word is "wash," as in "Please wash your pet."	
	What's the clue?	w a <u>s h</u>
brush -	Underline U-S-H.	<u>u s h</u>
	What's the family?	u s h
	What's the word?	b r u s h
food -	If you pet is hungry, you must give him some -	f o o d
	What's the clue?	f <u>o o</u> d
me ow -	We had this word and this sound. Can you read them?	m e o w
meow -	What' sound does a cat make?	m e o w
white -	Underline I-T-E.	<u>i t e</u>
	What's the family?	i t e
	What's the word?	w h i t e

	Teacher:	**Student:**
rabbit -	Underline A-B.	<u>a b</u>
	What's the family?	a b
	Add "r."	r a b
	Underline I - T.	<u>i t</u>
	What's the family?	i t
	Add "b."	b i t
	What's the word?	r a b b i t
high -	Underline I-G-H.	i <u>g h</u>
	What's the sight family?	i g h
	What's the word?	h i g h
lot -	Underline O-T.	<u>o t</u>
	What's the family?	o t
	What's the word?	l o t
lots -	What's the next word?	l o t s
	Underline "s."	l o t <u>s</u>
love -	This word is "love," as in "I <u>love</u> my pet."	
	What's the clue?	l o <u>v</u> e

<u>Pages 108 - 114</u>

different -	Underline I-F.	<u>i f</u>
	What's the family?	i f
	Add "d."	d i f
	Underline E-R.	<u>e r</u>
	What's the sight family?	e r
	Add "f."	f e r
	Underline E-N-T.	<u>e n t</u>
	What's the family?	e n t
	GO BACK - What's the word?	d i f f e r e n t
play -	We had this word. Can you read it?	p l a y
ground -	Underline O-U--N-D.	<u>o u n d</u>
	What's the sight family?	o u n d
	What's the word?	g r o u n d
playground -	What's the compound word?	p l a y g r o u n d
lunch -	Underline U-N-C-H.	<u>u n c h</u>
	What's the family?	u n c h
	What's the word?	l u n c h
slide -	Underline I-D-E.	i d e
	What's the family?	i d e
	What's the word?	s l i d e
it -	We had this word. Can you read it?	i t
it's -	What's the contraction?	i t ' s
sight -	Underline I-G-H-T.	<u>i g h t</u>
	What's the sight family?	i g h t
	What's the word?	s i g h t

	Teacher:	**Student:**
see saw -	We had these words. Can you read them?	s e e saw
seesaw -	What's the compound word?	s e e s a w
squirrel -	This word is "squirrel," as in "A <u>squirrel</u> likes nuts."	
	What's the clue?	<u>squirrel</u>
	(**Note:** Explain that "**qu**" always goes together.)	
swing -	Underline I-N-G.	<u>**i n g**</u>
	What's the family?	i n g
	What's the word?	s w i n g
traffic -	Underline A-F.	<u>**a f**</u>
	What's the family?	a f
	Add "tr."	t r a f
	Underline I-C.	<u>**i c**</u>
	What's the family?	i c
	Add "f."	f i c
	What's the word?	t r a f f i c
cop -	Underline O-P.	<u>**o p**</u>
	What's the family?	o p
	What's the word?	c o p
with out -	We had these words. Can you read them?	w i t h o u t
without -	What's the compound word?	w i t h o u t

Pages 115 - 120

show -	This word is "show," as in "We are going to see a <u>show</u>."	
	What's the clue?	s h <u>o</u> w
Miss -	Underline I-S-S.	<u>**i s s**</u>
	What's the family?	i s s
	What's the word?	M i s s
children -	Underline I-L.	<u>**i l**</u>
	What's the family?	i l
	Add "ch."	c h i l
	Underline E-N.	<u>**e n**</u>
	What's the family?	ǝ n
	Add "dr."	d r ǝ n
	What's the word?	c h i l d r ǝ n
school -	We learn how to read at -	s c h o o l
	What's the clue?	s c h <u>o o</u> l
puppet -	Underline U-P.	<u>**u p**</u>
	What's the family?	ᴜ p
	Add "p."	p ᴜ p
	Underline E-T.	<u>**e t**</u>
	What's the family?	e t
	Add "p."	p e t
	What's the word?	p u p p e t

	Teacher:	**Student:**
clap -	Underline A-P.	<u>a p</u>
	What's the family?	a p
	What's the word?	c l a p
round -	Underline O-U-N-D.	<u>o u n d</u>
	What's the sight family?	o u n d
	What's the word?	r o u n d
rock -	Underline O-C-K.	<u>o c k</u>
	What's the family?	o c k
	What's the word?	r o c k
sing -	Underline I-N-G.	<u>i n g</u>
	What's the family?	i n g
	What's the word?	s i n g
smile -	Underline I-L-E.	<u>i l e</u>
	What's the family?	i l e
	What's the word?	s m i l e

* *